Piano Sketches

Duets

Vitalij Neugasimov

T0086846

Book 2

5 easy to intermediate pieces for piano four-hands

Contents

	Level (approx. ABRSM grade)		Page
	Primo	Secondo	
Tarantella	3	3	2
Russian Song	3	4	8
Music for a Silent Film	4	5	12
Autumn in Paris	4	5	18
Rumba for Johann	5	5	22

Durations are given below each piece.

OXFORD
UNIVERSITY PRESS

Great Clarendon Street, Oxford OX2 6DP, United Kingdom

This collection © Oxford University Press 2017
Unauthorized arrangement or photocopying of this copyright material is ILLEGAL

Vitalij Neugasimov has asserted his right under the Copyright, Designs and Patents Act, 1988, to be identified as the Composer of these Works

Impression: 1
ISBN 978–0–19–351766–0
Music and text origination by Katie Johnston
Printed in Great Britain on acid-free paper by Halstan & Co. Ltd, Amersham, Bucks.

Thank you so much to my sister Liudmila Neugasimova, an exceptional piano teacher, for her invaluable contribution, brilliant ideas, encouragement, and support.

Tarantella

Vitalij Neugasimov

* Players with small hands may wish to omit the upper octave.

© Oxford University Press 2017. Photocopying this copyright material is ILLEGAL.

Tarantella

Vitalij Neugasimov

Duration: c.2 mins

© Oxford University Press 2017. Photocopying this copyright material is ILLEGAL.

19
dim.
mf più cantabile
mp
23
27
f marcato
30
33
ff
f

19
23
3
mf più cantabile
27
f
30
33
ff
f

37
f
mf
41
45
49
53
sf
8vb

37
8va
f
41
(8va)
sf
45
(8va)
sf
49
(8va)
sf
53
(8va)
sf

Russian Song

Vitalij Neugasimov

* Players with small hands may wish to omit the lower F.

© Oxford University Press 2017. Photocopying this copyright material is ILLEGAL.

Russian Song

Vitalij Neugasimov

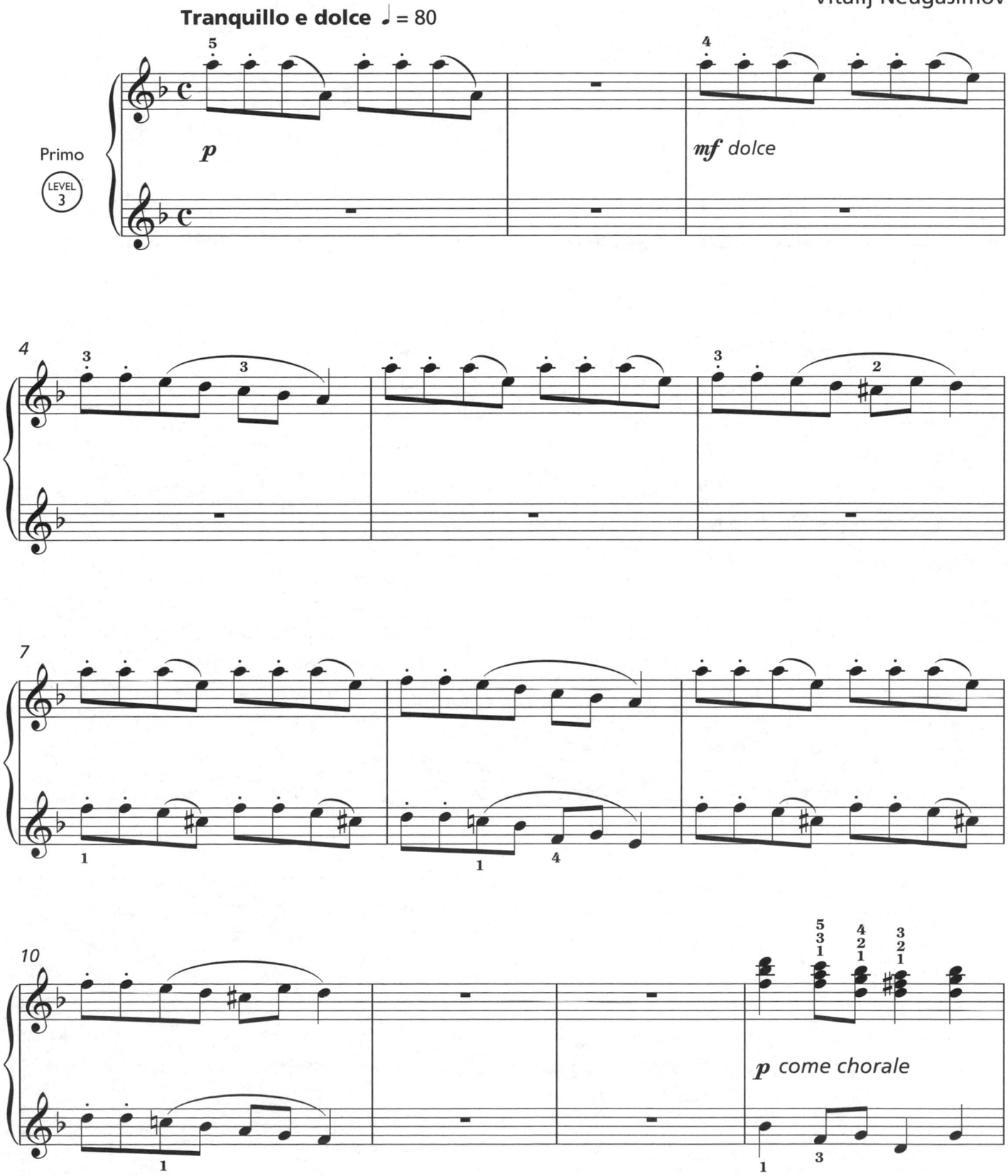

Duration: c.1.5 mins

© Oxford University Press 2017. Photocopying this copyright material is ILLEGAL.

14
mf
8vb
mf agitato
18
21
mf tranquillo
p
25
28
poco rit.
mf

* Players with small hands may wish to omit the lower F.

Music for a Silent Film

© Oxford University Press 2017. Photocopying this copyright material is ILLEGAL.

Music for a Silent Film

Vitalij Neugasimov

Duration: *c.*2 mins

© Oxford University Press 2017. Photocopying this copyright material is ILLEGAL.

17
p
21
25
29
33
mf
37

17
mf
21
25
29
33
f
37

41
p
45
49
mf
53
57
61
sf

41
mf
45
49
53
57
8va
mf tenuto la melodia
61
(8va)
sf

Autumn in Paris

© Oxford University Press 2017. Photocopying this copyright material is ILLEGAL.

Autumn in Paris

Vitalij Neugasimov

Duration: c.2.5 mins

© Oxford University Press 2017. Photocopying this copyright material is ILLEGAL.

29
mp più dolce
35
41
senza rit.
dim.
p semplice e comodo
48
rit.
a tempo
pp
cresc.
55
mp
62
69
colla Primo
calando

29
più dolce
35
41
senza rit.
dim.
p semplice e comodo
48
rit.
a tempo
55
mf come prima
62
69
a piacere (come cadenza)
pp

to my dearest friend Vytautas

Rumba for Johann

Vitalij Neugasimov

© Oxford University Press 2017. Photocopying this copyright material is ILLEGAL.

to my dearest friend Vytautas

Rumba for Johann

Vitalij Neugasimov

Duration: c.2 mins

© Oxford University Press 2017. Photocopying this copyright material is ILLEGAL.

21
mp
mf
25
mf
29
33
f
mf
37
mp
p
41

21
25
29
f
33
mf
37
mp
più cantabile
41

45
mf
49
f
53
mf
57
mp cresc.
61
f
65
marcato
ff

45
f
49
ff
53
57
tr
mf
cresc.
61
f
65
marcato
ff